MONEY MATTERS!

Types of Money

by Mari Schuh

BELLWETHER MEDIA • MINNEAPOLIS, MN

BLASTOFF!
2
READERS

Note to Librarians, Teachers, and Parents:

Blastoff! Readers are carefully developed by literacy experts and combine standards-based content with developmentally appropriate text.

Level 1 provides the most support through repetition of high-frequency words, light text, predictable sentence patterns, and strong visual support.

Level 2 offers early readers a bit more challenge through varied simple sentences, increased text load, and less repetition of high-frequency words.

Level 3 advances early-fluent readers toward fluency through increased text and concept load, less reliance on visuals, longer sentences, and more literary language.

Level 4 builds reading stamina by providing more text per page, increased use of punctuation, greater variation in sentence patterns, and increasingly challenging vocabulary.

Level 5 encourages children to move from "learning to read" to "reading to learn" by providing even more text, varied writing styles, and less familiar topics.

Whichever book is right for your reader, Blastoff! Readers are the perfect books to build confidence and encourage a love of reading that will last a lifetime!

This edition first published in 2016 by Bellwether Media, Inc.

No part of this publication may be reproduced in whole or in part without written permission of the publisher. For information regarding permission, write to Bellwether Media, Inc., Attention: Permissions Department, 5357 Penn Avenue South, Minneapolis, MN 55419.

Library of Congress Cataloging-in-Publication Data

Schuh, Mari C., 1975-
   Types of Money / by Mari Schuh.
      pages cm. – (Blastoff! Readers: Money Matters)
   Summary: "Relevant images match informative text in this introduction to types of money. Intended for students in kindergarten through third grade"– Provided by publisher.
   Audience: Ages 5-8
   Audience: K to grade 3
   Includes bibliographical references and index.
   ISBN 978-1-62617-249-4 (hardcover: alk. paper)
   1. Money–Juvenile literature. I. Title.
   HG221.5.S38 2016
   332.4'04–dc23
                          2015001382

Table of Contents

How do people pay for things they **need** and **want**? They use money.

Money pays for **goods** and **services**. Money has **value** because people agree on what it is **worth**.

beads

beans

shells

stones

Long ago, people used beads, beans, and salt as money. They also used shells, stones, and metals.

Today, most countries have their own kind of money. A country's money is called its **currency**.

Cash is made up of coins and bills.

AMERICAN COINS

1¢ penny

5¢ nickel

10¢ dime

25¢ quarter

50¢ half dollar

$1 one dollar

Pennies, nickels, dimes, and quarters are common American coins.

AMERICAN BILLS

$1   one dollar

$2   two dollars

$5   five dollars

$10   ten dollars

$20   twenty dollars

$50   fifty dollars

$100   one hundred dollars

Bills are made of paper. The smallest U.S. bill is one dollar, or $1. The biggest is $100.

People have **checking accounts** at their **bank**.

They write **checks** to other people, companies, and stores.

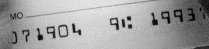

SLADJ
HO
OAK

70-477/719
71569971

MO ⑆071904 9⑈ 1993⑆

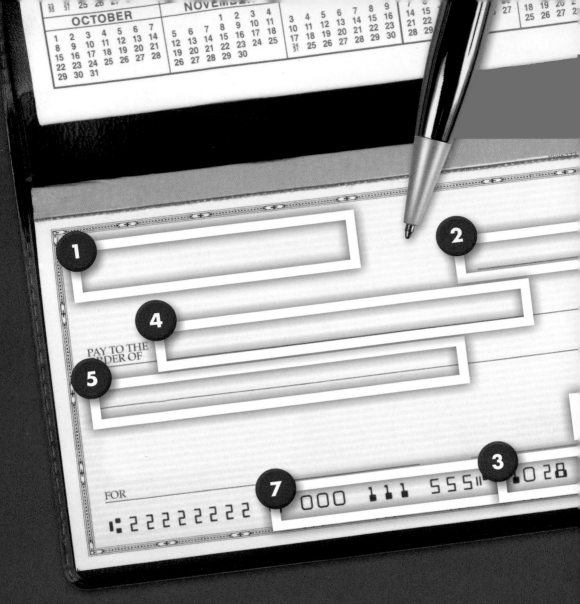

OCTOBER
1	2	3	4	5	6	7
8	9	10	11	12	13	14
15	16	17	18	19	20	21
22	23	24	25	26	27	28
29	30	31				

PAY TO THE
ORDER OF

FOR

⑦ ⑤ ⑧ 555 028

Eventually a check is **cashed** for money. It can also be **deposited** into another account.

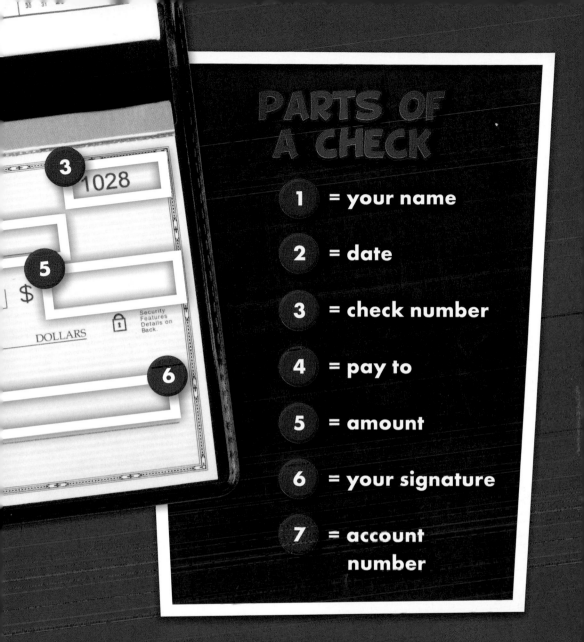

PARTS OF A CHECK

1 = your name

2 = date

3 = check number

4 = pay to

5 = amount

6 = your signature

7 = account number

The money is taken out of the payer's account.

Credit Cards

Credit cards let people borrow money to buy things right away. Then they pay for them later.

Credit cards are helpful for buying costly items.

PARTS OF A CREDIT CARD

1 = account number   **2** = your name

Credit card payments are
due every month.

People who cannot pay the full amount pay extra money later. This money is called **interest**.

Using Money Wisely

People should use their money for their needs first. Then extra money can be for wants.

COMMON NEEDS

food   clothes   school supplies

COMMON WANTS

games   toys   treats

People should try to stay out of **debt**. It is best to be smart with money!

Glossary

bank—a business where people keep their money

cashed—brought to a bank and traded for cash

checking accounts—supplies of personal money at banks

checks—printed pieces of paper people use to buy things; after a person writes a check, the bank takes money out of the person's checking account to make the payment.

credit cards—plastic cards people use to borrow money to buy things right away and pay for them later

currency—the kind of money a country uses

debt—money that a person owes

deposited—put into a bank account

goods—things that can be bought and sold

interest—extra money that is owed for borrowing money

need—must have to live

services—work that helps others

value—the amount that something is worth

want—would like to have

worth—the amount something is equal to

To Learn More

AT THE LIBRARY
Mooney, Carla. *Understanding Credit*. Minneapolis,
Minn.: Lerner Publications, 2015.

Reina, Mary. *Learn About Money*. North Mankato,
Minn.: Capstone Press, 2015.

Schwartz, Heather E. *Save Wisely*. Mankato, Minn.:
Amicus, 2016.

ON THE WEB
Learning more about types of
money is as easy as 1, 2, 3.

1. Go to www.factsurfer.com.

2. Enter "types of money" into the search box.

3. Click the "Surf" button and you will see a
   list of related web sites.

With factsurfer.com, finding more
information is just a click away.

Index